# SEA CREATURES AND FLYING REPTILES

Clare Hibbert

**Enslow Publishing**
101 W. 23rd Street
Suite 240
New York, NY 10011
USA
enslow.com

Published in 2019 by Enslow Publishing, LLC
101 W. 23rd Street, Suite 240, New York, NY 10011

**Cataloging-in-Publication Data**

Names: Hibbert, Clare.
Title: Sea Creatures and Flying Reptiles / Clare Hibbert.
Description: New York : Enslow Publishing, 2019. | Series: Dino explorers | Includes glossary and index.
Identifiers: ISBN 9780766099937 (pbk.) | ISBN 9780766099920 (library bound) | ISBN 9780766099951 (6 pack.) | ISBN 9780766099944 (ebook)
Subjects: LCSH: Marine reptiles, Fossil--Juvenile literature. | Pterosauria--Juvenile literature.
Classification: LCC QE861.5 H53 2019 | DDC 567.9'37--dc23

Printed in the United States of America

**To Our Readers:** We have done our best to make sure all website addresses in this book were active and appropriate when we went to press. However, the author and the publisher have no control over and assume no liability for the material available on those websites or on any websites they may link to. Any comments or suggestions can be sent by email to customerservice@enslow.com.

Excerpts and articles have been reproduced with the permission of the copyright holders.

# CONTENTS

# The Dinosaur Age

Dinosaurs appeared around 225 million years ago (mya) and ruled the land for over 160 million years. At the same time (the Mesozoic Era), marine reptiles and pterosaurs ruled the oceans and skies.

**Dinosaurs**

This family tree shows when various dinosaurs appeared and how they were related. As new fossils are found, paleontologists often change their minds about the groupings.

Dinosaurs suddenly died out 65 mya, along with marine reptiles, pterosaurs and many other animals. A huge meteorite probably hit Earth, throwing up dust that blocked out the Sun for months.

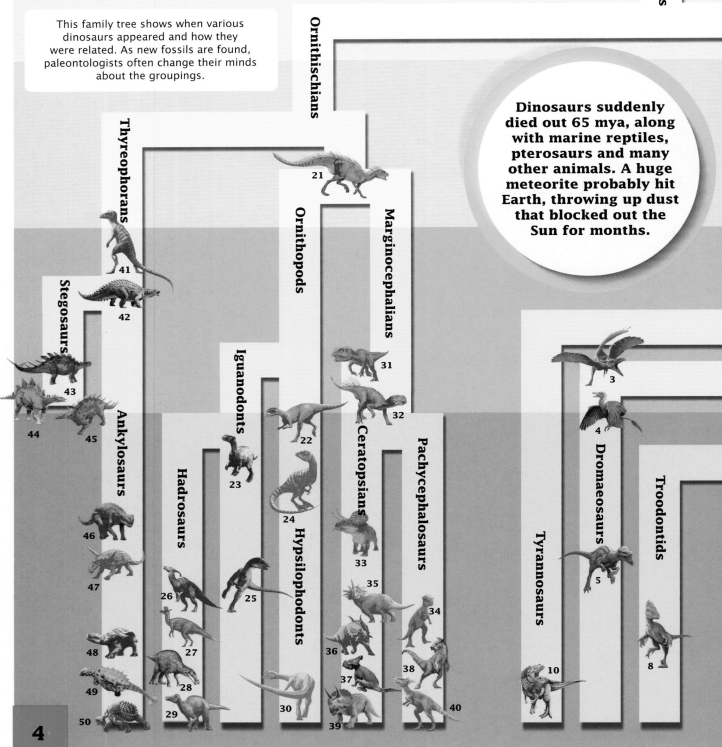

Ornithischians

Thyreophorans

Ornithopods

Marginocephalians

Stegosaurs

Iguanodonts

Ankylosaurs

Hadrosaurs

Hypsilophodonts

Ceratopsians

Pachycephalosaurs

Tyrannosaurs

Dromaeosaurs

Troodontids

**KEY**

1. *Herrerasaurus*
2. *Allosaurus*
3. *Archaeopteryx*
4. *Microraptor*
5. *Deinonychus*
6. *Spinosaurus*
7. *Giganotosaurus*
8. *Troodon*
9. *Therizinosaurus*
10. *Tyrannosaurus*
11. *Melanorosaurus*
12. *Plateosaurus*
13. *Mamenchisaurus*
14. *Brachiosaurus*
15. *Amargasaurus*
16. *Nigersaurus*
17. *Sauroposeidon*
18. *Argentinosaurus*
19. *Saltasaurus*
20. *Rapetosaurus*
21. *Heterodontosaurus*
22. *Hypsilophodon*
23. *Iguanodon*
24. *Leaellynasaura*
25. *Gasparinisaura*
26. *Parasaurolophus*
27. *Lambeosaurus*
28. *Shantungosaurus*
29. *Edmontosaurus*
30. *Thescelosaurus*
31. *Yinlong*
32. *Psittacosaurus*
33. *Zuniceratops*
34. *Stegoceras*
35. *Styracosaurus*
36. *Achelousaurus*
37. *Protoceratops*
38. *Pachycephalosaurus*
39. *Triceratops*
40. *Stygimoloch*
41. *Scutellosaurus*
42. *Scelidosaurus*
43. *Tuojiangosaurus*
44. *Stegosaurus*
45. *Kentrosaurus*
46. *Minmi*
47. *Sauropelta*
48. *Edmontonia*
49. *Euoplocephalus*
50. *Ankylosaurus*

Saurischians
Theropods
Allosaurs
Spinosaurs
Therizinosaurs
Sauropods
Prosauropods
Diplodocids
Titanosaurs
1
2
7
9
11
12
13
14
15
16
17
18
19
20
47
Triassic
251–206 mya
Jurassic
206–145 mya
Cretaceous
145-65 mya

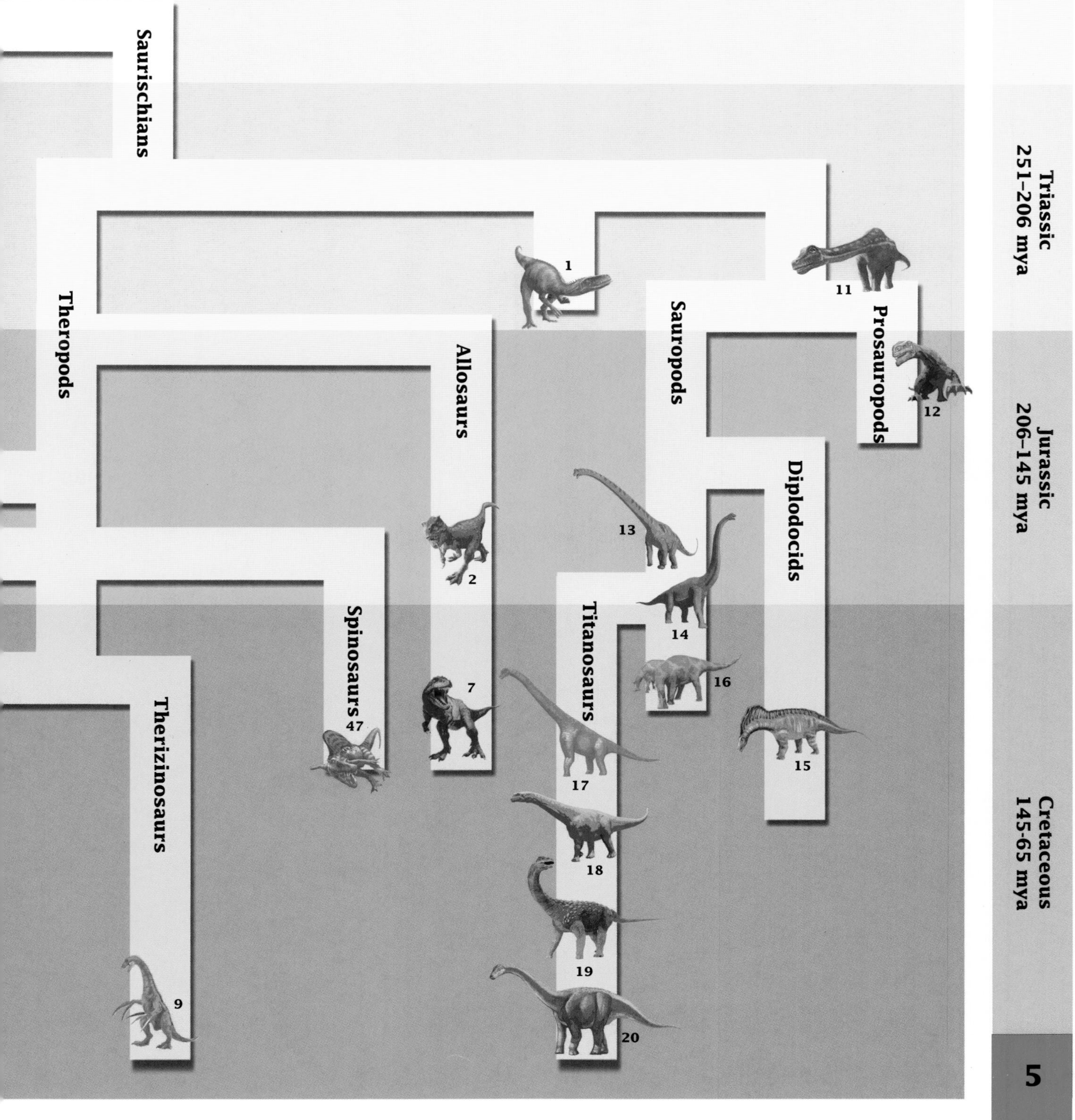

# Plesiosaurus

Many types of reptile lived in Mesozoic oceans. The plesiosaurs were a group of long-necked swimming reptiles that first appeared in the Late Triassic and died out at the end of the Cretaceous. They are named after *Plesiosaurus* (the "close lizard").

## Life in the Water

*Plesiosaurus* lived in shallow waters, close to the coast. It's possible it came ashore to lay its eggs, like today's turtles. It could not have moved quickly on land, because it had flippers instead of legs. Plesiosaurs evolved from nothosaurs, Triassic, four-legged reptiles whose feet had adapted to swimming in the water by being webbed and paddle-like.

*Kaiwhekea* was one of the last plesiosaurs. A specialist squid hunter, it grew to 23 feet (7 m) long.

*Meyerasaurus* lived in the Early Jurassic. It was about the same length as *Plesiosaurus*.

## Short-Necked Cousins

Not all plesiosaurs had long necks. Pliosaurs, including *Pliosaurus* (page 10), *Kronosaurus* (pages 10–11) and *Meyerasaurus*, were plesiosaurs with shorter necks and bigger heads. Pliosaurs also had slightly larger back flippers than front ones (in most plesiosaurs, the front flippers were larger). However, all plesiosaurs shared the same feeding technique—snapping up fish and squid as they moved their head from side to side.

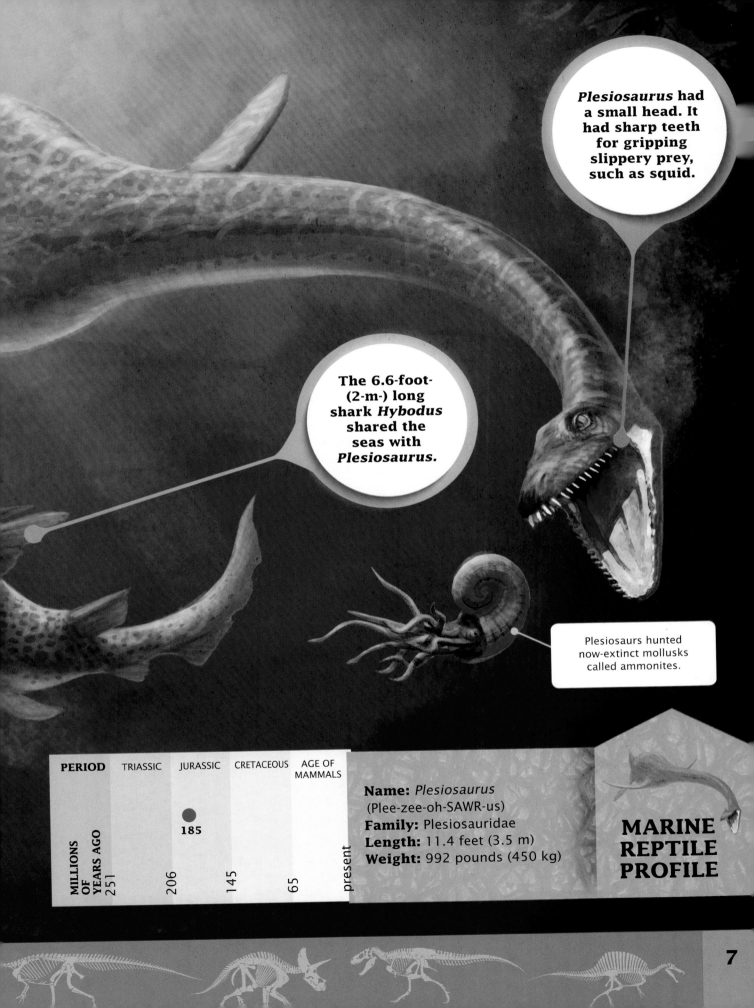

*Plesiosaurus* had a small head. It had sharp teeth for gripping slippery prey, such as squid.

The 6.6-foot- (2-m-) long shark *Hybodus* shared the seas with *Plesiosaurus.*

Plesiosaurs hunted now-extinct mollusks called ammonites.

| PERIOD | TRIASSIC | JURASSIC | CRETACEOUS | AGE OF MAMMALS |
|---|---|---|---|---|
| MILLIONS OF YEARS AGO | | ● 185 | | |
| 251 | 206 | 145 | 65 | present |

**Name:** *Plesiosaurus* (Plee-zee-oh-SAWR-us)
**Family:** Plesiosauridae
**Length:** 11.4 feet (3.5 m)
**Weight:** 992 pounds (450 kg)

**MARINE REPTILE PROFILE**

# Temnodontosaurus

Streamlined like dolphins and usually fast-moving, ichthyosaurs were large marine reptiles that first appeared in the Late Triassic and survived until the Late Cretaceous. *Temnodontosaurus* was one of the biggest ichthyosaurs, at 39 feet (12 m) long. Most species were around 9.8 feet (3 m) long.

## Air, Land, and Sea

Ichthyosaurs had to come up for air because they could not breathe underwater—but they did not need to come ashore to lay their eggs. Like some snakes today, ichthyosaurs were viviparous. In other words, their eggs developed inside their body and then the animals gave birth to live young.

The small, sharp teeth were perfectly suited for gripping slippery fish.

*Shonisaurus* was massive and slow-moving. Unlike most ichthyosaurs, it did not have a dorsal (back) fin.

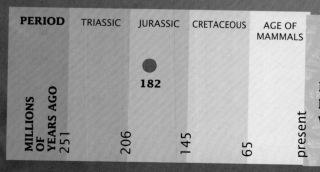

| PERIOD | TRIASSIC | JURASSIC | CRETACEOUS | AGE OF MAMMALS |
|--------|----------|----------|------------|----------------|
| MILLIONS OF YEARS AGO | 251 | ● 182 · 206 | 145 | 65 · present |

**Name:** *Temnodontosaurus*
(Tem-noh-DON-tuh-SAWR-us)
**Family:** Temnodontosauridae
**Length:** 39 feet (12 m)
**Weight:** 5 tons (4.5 t)

**MARINE REPTILE PROFILE**

Like most ichthyosaurs, *Temnodontosaurus* swam at high speeds. It moved its tail from side to side to propel itself through the water.

## Hunting Accessories

*Temnodontosaurus*'s name means "cutting tooth lizard." Its long, narrow jaw was packed with small, sharp teeth. However, this ichthyosaur is better-known for its huge eyes. In one species, *Temnodontosaurus platyodon*, these were 8 inches (20 cm) across.

**Temnodontosaurus's enormous eyes let in plenty of light, allowing the hunter to see in the ocean gloom.**

Cast of *Temnodontosaurus platyodon*'s skull.

# Kronosaurus

One of the largest pliosaurs, 33-foot- (10-m-) long *Kronosaurus* lived in the Early Cretaceous. It powered through the water after turtles and other plesiosaurs, snapping them up in its huge jaws.

## Built for Speed

Pliosaurs had muscular bodies, short necks, and long heads. The short tail kept them streamlined and they swam by moving all four flippers at once. They were fast-moving and usually outswam prey. Once they had caught their victim, they shook it in their jaws and swallowed it whole.

Pliosaurs are named after the Late Jurassic marine reptile *Pliosaurus*.

*Kronosaurus's* teeth were not very sharp, but they were good at gripping and crushing prey.

The pointed tail helped the body slip through the water without creating any drag.

## History of Discovery

The first *Kronosaurus* fossils—teeth dug up in Australia in 1899—were not identified as *Kronosaurus* until the 1920s. For decades the pliosaur was known only to have lived in Australia. In 1994, paleontologists announced that a fossil had been found in Colombia, South America. *Kronosaurus* probably lived in shallow seas worldwide.

Pliosaurs "flew" through the water using their four wing-like flippers.

*Kronosaurus*'s longest teeth were around 12 inches (30 cm) long. Even the shortest were nearly 3 inches (7 cm).

| PERIOD | TRIASSIC | JURASSIC | CRETACEOUS | AGE OF MAMMALS |
|---|---|---|---|---|
| MILLIONS OF YEARS AGO | 251 | 206 | 145 ● 112 | 65 present |

**Name:** *Kronosaurus* (KROH-nuh-SAWR-us)
**Family:** Pliosauridae
**Length:** 33 feet (10 m)
**Weight:** 9 tons (8.2 t)

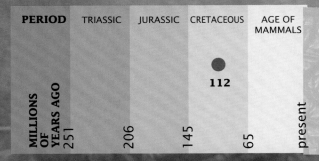

## MARINE REPTILE PROFILE

# Albertonectes

The elasmosaurs were plesiosaurs that had incredibly long necks. *Albertonectes* ("Alberta swimmer") had the longest neck of any elasmosaur, and the greatest overall body length of any plesiosaur.

## Sneaky Skills

*Albertonectes* was not a fast swimmer, but it had a clever hunting technique. It approached shoals of fish from below, then let its head spring up on its long neck like a jack-in-the-box. This took the fish completely by surprise, so *Albertonectes* could gulp plenty down before they swam away.

*Albertonectes'* neck was about 23 feet (7 m) long—half of its total body length.

## Long-Necked Family

Elasmosaurs are named after the Late Cretaceous plesiosaur *Elasmosaurus*, but may have been around from the Late Triassic. Early elasmosaurs were just 9.8 feet (3 m) long. Elasmosaur means "thin-plated lizard" and refers to the thin plates in the reptiles' pelvic girdles.

*Elasmosaurus* had stones called gastroliths in its stomach to help it digest its food.

*Albertonectes* had a flat skull and long, pointed teeth.

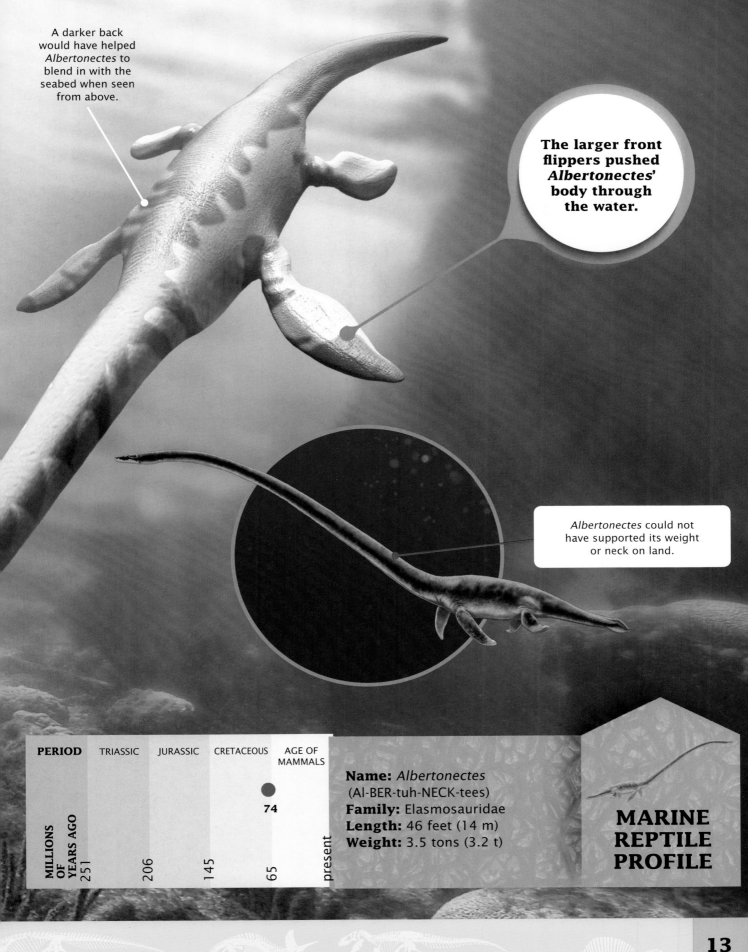

A darker back would have helped *Albertonectes* to blend in with the seabed when seen from above.

The larger front flippers pushed *Albertonectes'* body through the water.

*Albertonectes* could not have supported its weight or neck on land.

| PERIOD | TRIASSIC | JURASSIC | CRETACEOUS | AGE OF MAMMALS |
|--------|----------|----------|------------|----------------|
| MILLIONS OF YEARS AGO | 251 | 206 | 145 | 65 | present |

74

**Name:** *Albertonectes*
(Al-BER-tuh-NECK-tees)
**Family:** Elasmosauridae
**Length:** 46 feet (14 m)
**Weight:** 3.5 tons (3.2 t)

## MARINE REPTILE PROFILE

# Mosasaurus

The mosasaurs were the apex marine predators in the Late Cretaceous. They are named after *Mosasaurus*, a 59-foot- (18-m-) long hunter that went after fish, turtles, plesiosaurs, ichthyosaurs, and even smaller mosasaurs.

The scales on the skin were tiny, making *Mosasaurus* smooth and streamlined.

## All in the Family

The smallest mosasaurs were less than 3.3 feet (1 m) long. Like *Mosasaurus*, they had lizard-shaped bodies and long, broad tails that helped to propel them through the water. Another family characteristic was giving birth to live young, rather than coming ashore to lay eggs.

### Early Discoveries

The first known mosasaur remains were fragments of *Mosasaurus* skull found in the 1760s near Maastricht, in the Netherlands. It was mistaken for a toothed whale, and not identified as a reptile until 1799. The animal was finally named in 1822: *Mosasaurus* means "Maas River lizard," referring to the river that flows through the city of Maastricht.

The first *Mosasaurus* fossil was found in a chalk quarry.

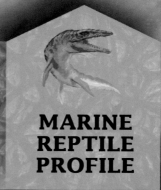

| PERIOD | TRIASSIC | JURASSIC | CRETACEOUS | AGE OF MAMMALS |
|--------|----------|----------|------------|----------------|
| MILLIONS OF YEARS AGO | 251 | 206 | 145 | 65 · present |

68

**Name:** *Mosasaurus*
(MOH-suh-SAWR-us)
**Family:** Mosasauridae
**Length:** 59 feet (18 m)
**Weight:** 5.5 tons (5 t)

**MARINE REPTILE PROFILE**

The skull was 5.6 feet (1.7 m) long—about the length of a car.

*Mosasaurus* had a double-hinged jaw, like a snake's, that could open wide to swallow prey whole.

Five *Mosasaurus* species have been identified. This skull belongs to *Mosasaurus lemonnieri*, discovered in 1889.

*Mosasaurus's* paddle-like limbs each had five digits.

# Dimorphodon

The pterosaurs, or "winged lizards," were flying reptiles that appeared in the Late Triassic, around 200 mya. *Dimorphodon* was an average-sized pterosaur that lived during the Early Jurassic. Its head looked like a puffin's.

## Coastal Lifestyle

*Dimorphodon* could fly, but not for long distances. It probably lived along coasts, climbing cliffs or moving around on all fours. It caught its main food—insects— by snapping its jaws shut very fast. It also ate fish, small animals, and carrion.

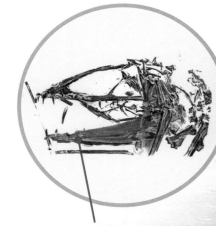

This drawing of *Dimorphodon*'s skull appeared in Richard Owen's *A History of British Fossil Reptiles* (1849–84).

## Wings and Flight

Pterosaurs were the first vertebrates (animals with backbones) that were capable of powered flight. Their wings, which were made of skin, muscle, and other tissues, stretched from their long fourth finger down to their ankles.

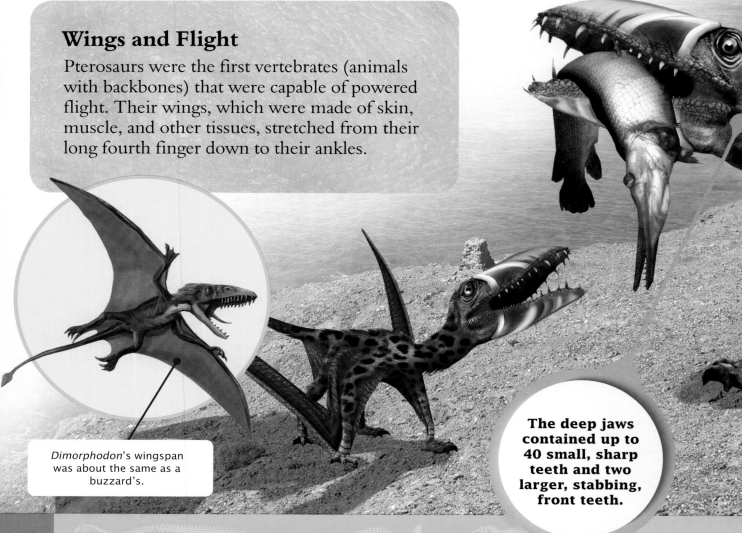

*Dimorphodon*'s wingspan was about the same as a buzzard's.

The deep jaws contained up to 40 small, sharp teeth and two larger, stabbing, front teeth.

**Name:** *Dimorphodon*
(Dye-MAW-fuh-don)
**Family:** Dimorphodontidae
**Length:** 3.3 feet (1 m)
**Wingspan:** 4.6 feet (1.4 m)
**Weight:** 5 pounds (2.3 kg)

**PTEROSAUR PROFILE**

A diamond-shaped flap at the end of *Dimorphodon*'s tail helped it to steer when flying.

*Dimorphodon* may have cared for its young like this, or it may have left them to fend for themselves.

*Dimorphodon* had two types of teeth (its name means "two teeth shapes").

# Pterodactylus

Non-experts often use "pterodactyl" to mean any pterosaur, probably because *Pterodactylus* was the first-known pterosaur. It was discovered in Bavaria, Germany, in limestone formed in the Late Jurassic. More than 100 specimens have been found, many of them juveniles.

## Breeding Season

Paleontologists have identified *Pterodactylus* that are one, two, and three years old. Their finds show that the reptile had a set breeding season, timed so eggs hatched when the conditions were best for raising young. *Pterodactylus* probably nested in colonies, like many seabirds today.

**Pterodactylus was lightly built, with long wings. It would have been a powerful flier.**

*Pterodactylus* had a crest of soft tissue on the top of its head for display. It kept growing throughout its life.

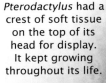

| PERIOD | TRIASSIC | JURASSIC | CRETACEOUS | AGE OF MAMMALS |
|---|---|---|---|---|
| | | ● 150 | | |
| MILLIONS OF YEARS AGO | 251 | 206 | 145 | 65 | present |

**Name:** *Pterodactylus*
(Ter-oh-DAK-til-us)
**Family:** Pterodactylidae
**Length:** 31.5 inches (80 cm)
**Wingspan:** 3.3 feet (1 m)
**Weight:** 10 pounds (4.5 kg)

**PTEROSAUR PROFILE**

# Early Fossil Finds

*Pterodactylus* was discovered in 1784, but not recognized as a flying reptile until 1812. Its name means "winged finger." As in all pterosaurs, *Pterodactylus*'s wing was made up of stretched skin, attached to its extra-long fourth finger.

When *Pterodactylus* dived for fish, the hair-like pycnofibers around its neck stopped it from getting cold and wet.

A young *Pterodactylus*, preserved in limestone.

The jaw contained up to 90 small, sharp teeth.

The wing was made up of skin and muscle.

# Tropeognathus

With a wingspan as long as a school bus, *Tropeognathus* was one of the largest-known pterosaurs. It lived off the coast of what is now South America during the Early Cretaceous.

## Spoon-Shaped Snout

*Tropeognathus* means "keel jaw." The name comes from the crests on the pterosaur's snout and lower jaw, which are shaped like keels (the steering fins on the bottom of a boat). The result is a curvy mouth that slides easily into the water to grab fish.

The rounded snout crests were probably used for display, to show off to possible mates or rivals.

The stretchy skin of the wing was supported by the pterosaur's long wrist bone and the long bones of the fourth finger.

| PERIOD | TRIASSIC | JURASSIC | CRETACEOUS | AGE OF MAMMALS |
|--------|----------|----------|------------|----------------|
| MILLIONS OF YEARS AGO | 251 | 206 | 145 ● 110 | 65 present |

**Name:** *Tropeognathus*
(TRO-pe-oh-NA-thus)
**Family:** Pterodactylidae
**Length:** 20 feet (6 m)
**Wingspan:** 27 feet (8.2 m)
**Weight:** 28 pounds (13 kg)

## PTEROSAUR PROFILE

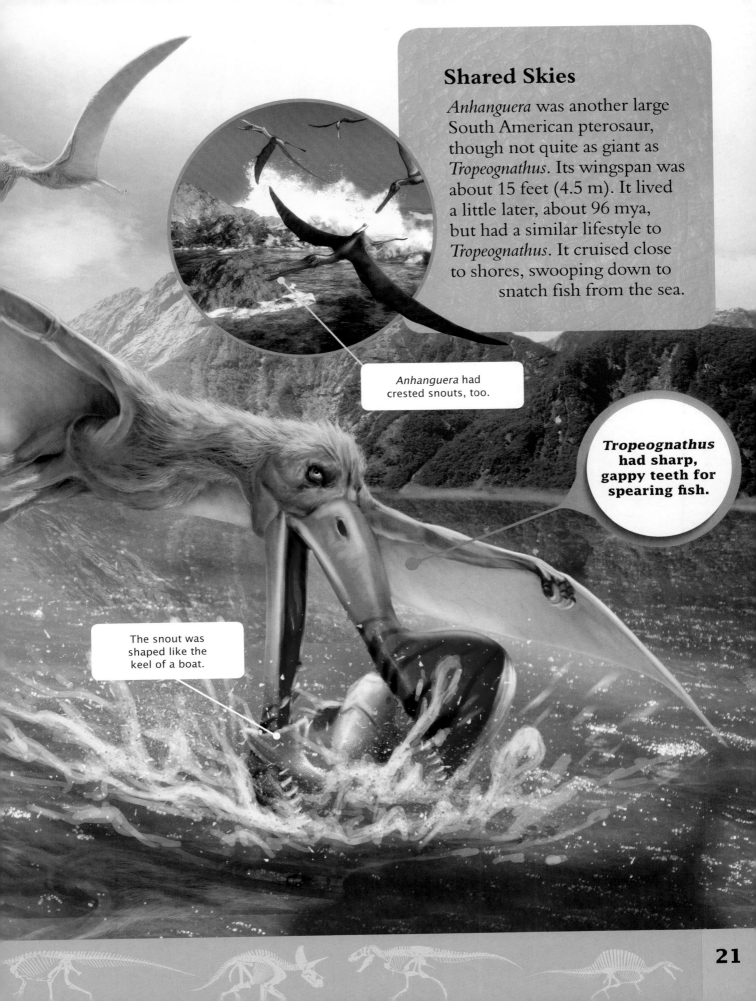

## Shared Skies

*Anhanguera* was another large South American pterosaur, though not quite as giant as *Tropeognathus*. Its wingspan was about 15 feet (4.5 m). It lived a little later, about 96 mya, but had a similar lifestyle to *Tropeognathus*. It cruised close to shores, swooping down to snatch fish from the sea.

*Anhanguera* had crested snouts, too.

**Tropeognathus had sharp, gappy teeth for spearing fish.**

The snout was shaped like the keel of a boat.

# Pteranodon

With its long, sharp beak and backward-pointing crest, the large pterosaur *Pteranodon* was the perfect shape for diving into the sea. It lived across what is now North America about 83 mya. It may also have lived in the area of Sweden, northern Europe.

## Feeding Technique

Earlier pterosaurs such as *Pterodactylus* (pages 18–19) had teeth in their jaws, but *Pteranodon* had a toothless beak (its name means "wing without tooth"). A powerful flier, *Pteranodon* could have fed by diving headfirst into the water like a gannet, by dipping for food as it flew low over the sea, or by swimming and snatching fish near the surface.

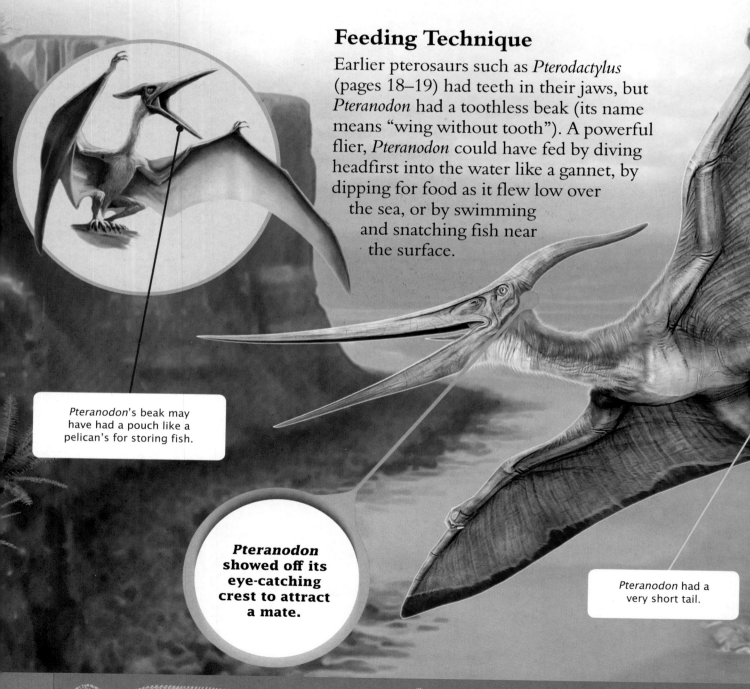

*Pteranodon*'s beak may have had a pouch like a pelican's for storing fish.

*Pteranodon* showed off its eye-catching crest to attract a mate.

*Pteranodon* had a very short tail.

## Unique Pterosaur

*Pteranodon* was the first pterosaur discovered outside Europe. Its wing bones were found in Kansas in 1870. Over the years, many different species were identified, but today most paleontologists agree that there was just one, *Pteranodon longiceps* (*longiceps* means "long-headed" and refers to the bony crest).

*Pteranodon* glided when it could, to save energy, but it also flapped its wings when it needed to put on a burst of speed.

*Pteranodon* walked quadrupedally (on all fours), rather than bipedally (upright on its back legs).

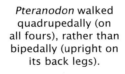

| PERIOD | TRIASSIC | JURASSIC | CRETACEOUS | AGE OF MAMMALS |
|---|---|---|---|---|
| | | | 83 | |
| MILLIONS OF YEARS AGO 251 | 206 | 145 | 65 | present |

**Name:** *Pteranodon* (Ter-AN-oh-don)
**Family:** Pteranodontidae
**Length:** 6 feet (1.8 m)
**Wingspan:** 20 feet (6 m)
**Weight:** 55 pounds (25 kg)

**PTEROSAUR PROFILE**

# Quetzalcoatlus

Named after Quetzalcoatl, the feathered serpent god of Aztec mythology, *Quetzalcoatlus* lived at the end of the Cretaceous. Its wingspan was up to 36 feet (11 m), making it the largest of the 150 known species of pterosaur.

## On the Lookout

*Quetzalcoatlus* had a long neck and good eyesight. On land it walked on all fours, looking for carrion or small animals to eat. Flight used a lot of energy. Wherever possible, *Quetzalcoatlus* glided rather than flapping its wings.

## Taking Off

Smaller pterosaurs could launch themselves into the air by running along on their back legs, like birds. Larger ones, such as *Quetzalcoatlus*, were too heavy for that and needed to start from a quadrupedal position. Their front legs were much stronger than their back ones, and could give enough of an upward thrust to make the animal airborne.

The wing membrane was thin but tough. The wings were 9 inches (23 cm) thick at the elbows.

Pterosaurs did not have feathers. However some, perhaps including *Quetzalcoatlus*, had fuzzy filaments called pycnofibers covering their bodies.

| PERIOD | TRIASSIC | JURASSIC | CRETACEOUS | AGE OF MAMMALS |
|---|---|---|---|---|

**MILLIONS OF YEARS AGO** 251 206 145 65 present

67

**Name:** *Quetzalcoatlus*
(Kwet-zel-KWAT-al-us)
**Family:** Azhdarchidae
**Height:** 16 feet (4.9 m)
**Wingspan:** 36 feet (11 m)
**Weight:** 496 pounds (225 kg)

## PTEROSAUR PROFILE

*Quetzalcoatlus* flew inland, rather than over the sea, so it could glide on thermals (currents of warm air).

**Quetzalcoatlus's narrow, toothless beak was at least 8 feet (2.4 m) long.**

The back legs were probably the first to touch the ground when *Quetzalcoatlus* landed.

# Fun Facts

Now that you have discovered some amazing prehistoric creatures, boost your knowledge with these 10 quick facts about them!

The 19th-century fossil collector Mary Anning found the first Plesiosaurus in southern England in 1821. It was an almost-complete skeleton.

The largest-known *ichthyosaur* is 69-foot (21-m) *Shastasaurus*.

*Kronosaurus* was named after Cronos, the leader of the Titans in Greek mythology. Cronos's son, Zeus, became the king of the gods.

*Albertonectes* is known from just one fossil—a complete skeleton that was found by miners. The discovery was announced in 2012.

Paleontologists cannot agree if *Mosasaurus* was more closely related to snakes or to monitor lizards.

Fossil collector Mary Anning found the first *Dimorphodon* fossils in Dorset, southern England, in 1828.

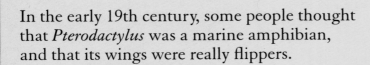

In the early 19th century, some people thought that *Pterodactylus* was a marine amphibian, and that its wings were really flippers.

*Tropeognathus* and *Anhanguera* were both ornithocheirids—pterosaurs with large wingspans that were specially adapted for flying out at sea.

More fossils have been found of *Pteranodon* than of any other pterosaur—at least 1,200 at the last count.

*Quetzalcoatlus* belonged to a family called the azhdarchids, which includes some of the largest flying animals of all time.

# Your Questions Answered

We know an incredible amount of facts about prehistoric creatures, even though they lived millions of years ago. Scientists are still finding out new details and unearthing fossils that teach us about the history of life on Earth. Every new discovery answers some questions and leads scientists to ask new ones. Here are some fascinating questions that scientists now know the answers to.

## Were prehistoric sharks similar to today's species?

Sharks have lived on Earth for millions of years. Some of today's sharks, such as shysharks, are called "living fossils" because they are still very similar to their ancestors who were alive about 150 million years ago! Scientists have also discovered that some types of shark used to migrate. *Bandringa* were alive about 300 million years ago. They swam from their river homes to the ocean to lay their eggs. To this day, sharks migrate during breeding season.

*A lemon shark pup in the safe, shallow waters of a mangrove forest. It will move to the open ocean once it is a larger, more experienced hunter.*

## What was the largest flying animal of all time?

The record for largest wingspan of any modern-day animal is held by a wandering albatross: 11.8 feet (3.6 m). The largest bird to have ever lived is *Pelagornis*. It was alive 25 million years ago and its wingspan measured 24.2 feet (7.4 m). However, the largest wingspan of any animal was 34 feet (10.4 m), belonging to *Quetzalcoatlus northropi*. This flying reptile lived about 68 million years ago.

## Were there any swimming dinosaurs?

All the swimming creatures in this book are prehistoric reptiles. Until recently, paleontologists hadn't found remains of a dinosaur that could swim, but that changed in 2014. On examining a well-preserved fossil of *Spinosaurus*, scientists confirmed that this was the first-known swimming dinosaur. *Spinosaurus* was probably the largest carnivorous dinosaur ever to have lived, measuring 52.5 feet (16 m) end-to-end.

*Spinosaurus was an excellent hunter. It fed on fish, as well as dinosaurs and other land animals.*

## Can feathers fossilize?

Feathers are made of keratin—the same material as our hair and nails. As such, they are much softer than bones. There are, however, rare and precious finds of fully preserved feathers: they have been sealed in prehistoric tree resin that has turned into amber over millions of years.

*The slow, oozing resin from tree bark can seal in wildlife, such as insects and beetles, too. It hardens over millions of years to become amber, preserving the wildlife inside it.*

## Did any swimming reptiles have blubber?

Reptiles are cold-blooded. This means that their body temperature is regulated by the temperature of the environment they are in. When scientists managed to calculate the body temperature of some ichthyosaurs (pages 8–9) and plesiosaurs (pages 6–7), however, they discovered something unusual. These prehistoric creatures had had a much higher body temperature than the waters they swam in. In order to keep their bodies warm while pursuing prey, ichthyosaurs and plesiosaurs may have had insulating blubber, like whales, seals, and many other marine mammals do today.

# Glossary

**ammonite**  An extinct Mesozoic shellfish with a coiled shell.

**azhdarchid**  A pterosaur with long legs, a long neck, and a huge wingspan.

**bipedal**  Walking upright on the back legs.

**carnivore**  A meat-eater.

**carrion**  Rotting flesh from a dead animal.

**Cretaceous period**  The time from 145 to 65 mya, and the third of the periods that make up the Mesozoic Era.

**extinct**  Describes an animal or plant that has disappeared forever.

**flipper**  A flat limb that has evolved to help an animal swim.

**fossil**  The remains of an animal or plant that died long ago, preserved in rock.

**gastrolith**  A stone in the stomach that helps digestion.

**ichthyosaur**  A dolphin-like, predatory marine reptile of the Mesozoic Era.

**Jurassic period**  The time from 206 to 145 mya, and the second of the periods that make up the Mesozoic Era.

**Mesozioc Era**  The period of geological time from 251 to 65 million years ago.

**mosasaur**  A large, predatory marine reptile of the Cretaceous, which had four paddle-like limbs.

**mya**  Short for "millions of years ago."

**nothosaur**  A marine reptile of the Triassic, with webbed, paddle-like feet.

**ornithocheirid**  A pterosaur with a huge wingspan and keel-shaped snout.

**paleontologist**  A scientist who studies fossils.

**plate**  A protective, bony section on a reptile's skin.

**plesiosaur**  A long-necked marine reptile that lived in the Jurassic and Cretaceous.

**pliosaur**  A kind of plesiosaur with a short neck and big head.

**predator**  An animal that hunts and eats other animals for food.

**prey**  An animal that is hunted and eaten by other animals for food.

**pterosaur**  A flying reptile with wings made from skin stretched over a long fourth finger.

**pycnofiber**  A hair-like body covering found on a pterosaur's body.

**quadrupedal**  Walking on all four legs.

**species**  One particular type of living thing. Members of the same species look similar and can produce offspring together.

**Triassic period**  The time from 251 to 206 mya, and the first of the periods that make up the Mesozoic Era.

**wingspan**  The width of a flying animal's outstretched wings, from wing tip to wing tip.

# Further Information

## BOOKS

Miles, Liz. *Flying Monsters.* New York, NY: Gareth Stevens Publishing, 2016.

Miles, Liz. *Sea Monsters.* New York, NY: Gareth Stevens Publishing, 2016.

Woodward, John. *Everything You Need to Know about Dinosaurs: and Other Prehistoric Creatures.* New York, NY: DK Publishing, 2014.

Woolf, Alex. *The Science of Sea Monsters: Prehistoric Reptiles of the Sea.* New York, NY: Franklin Watts, 2018.

## WEBSITES

**kids.nationalgeographic.com/animals/hubs/dinosaurs-and-prehistoric/**
Check out National Geographic Kids' info on dinosaurs and prehistoric animals.

**www.amnh.org/explore/ology/paleontology**
This paleontology website by the American Museum of Natural History is filled with quizzes, information, and activities!

**www.sciencenewsforstudents.org/search?tt=108**
Visit the Science News for Students website to find out about the latest science news. This link will take you straight to the section "Fossils," with all the most up-to-date information on discoveries by paleontologists.

# Index